Nail Fashion

Alison Hawes

Badger Publishing Limited
Oldmedow Road,
Hardwick Industrial Estate,
King's Lynn PE30 4JJ
Telephone: 01438 791037

www.badgerlearning.co.uk

2 4 6 8 10 9 7 5 3 1

Nail Fashion ISBN 978-1-78147- 821-9

Publisher: Susan Ross
Senior Editor: Danny Pearson
Publishing Assistant: Claire Morgan
Designer: Fiona Grant
Series Consultant: Dee Reid

The author would like to thank the staff of Tipz and Glitz of Worthing for all their help and advice.

Photos: Cover image: URBANLIP/Gallery Stock
Page 4: © aus-stock/iStock
Page 5: © Sumod Sunny/Alamy
Page 6: © Horizons WWP/Alamy
Page 7: John E. Kelly/Photodisc/Getty Images
Page 8: © imageBROKER/Alamy
Page 10: Paul Morton/E+/Getty Images
Page 12: © PLAINVIEW/iStock
Page 13: © MARKA/Alamy
Page 14: © Kumar Sriskandan/Alamy
Page 16: F1 Online/REX
Page 17: © Osuleo/iStock
Page 18: Lynn Koenig/Moment/Getty Images
Page 19: Image Source/REX
Page 20: Jodi Jacobson/E+/Getty Images
Page 21: Kris Hanke/E+/Getty Images
Page 22: Claude Guillaumin/Photographer's Choice/Getty Images,
Melanie Dawn Harter/Moment Open/Getty Images, Moment Open/Getty Images
Page 23: © Hightower_NRW/iStock
Page 24: © YAY Media AS/Alamy
Page 25: ICHIRO/The Image Bank/Getty Images
Page 26: David Thompson/REX
Page 28: © Semen Lihodeev/Alamy
Page 29: Ken McKay/REX
Page 30: © Colin Hawkins/Alamy

Attempts to contact all copyright holders have been made.
If any omitted would care to contact Badger Learning, we will be happy to make appropriate arrangements.

Contents

Vocabulary

ancient	fashion
cuticle	manicure
designs	metallic
Egypt	moisturise

1. Nail art long ago

Nail art is in fashion at the moment. But nail art is not new.

The first people to paint their fingernails lived in India over 5000 years ago. They were men and they painted their nails black!

Ancient Egypt

Long ago in Egypt, men and women painted their nails.

They used dye from the henna plant to colour their nails
a brown colour.

The nail colour they used showed how important they were.

Only the higher classes were allowed to use the colour red.

WOW! facts

Henna has been found on the nails of Egyptian mummies!

Ancient China

In ancient China, rich people grew their nails long to show they did not have to work with their hands.

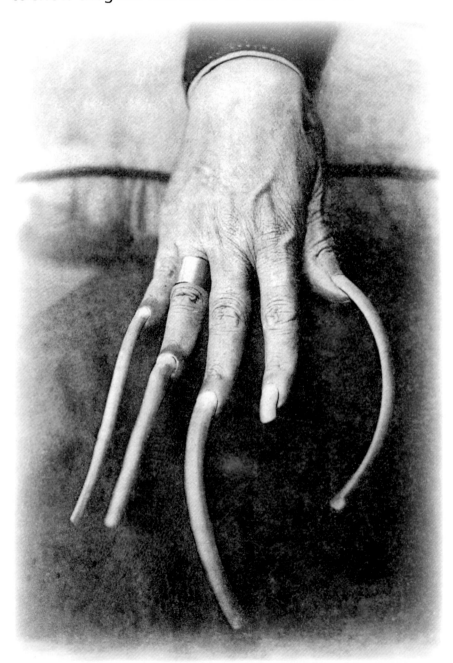

They also painted their nails.

The colour people used showed how important
they were.

Nail colour	Status	Meaning
Gold or silver	Very important people	Power
Red or black	Important people	Strength
Pale colours	Ordinary people	Weakness

WOW! facts

The ancient Chinese made nail polish
from beeswax, egg white and plant dye!

2. Nail art today

Modern nail polish was invented in 1917.

It was developed from the paint used on cars!

The first nail polish was clear. Later, pink, red, purple and black polishes were made.

Now nail polish comes in just about every colour you can think of!

Special polishes

As well as ordinary nail polish, there are some special nail polishes available.

Type of polish	Colour	Used because
Base coat	**Clear**	• it strengthens nails and stops coloured polish staining nails
Gel polish	**Coloured**	• it lasts twice as long as ordinary nail polish
Top coat	**Clear**	• it stops nail polish chipping and peeling

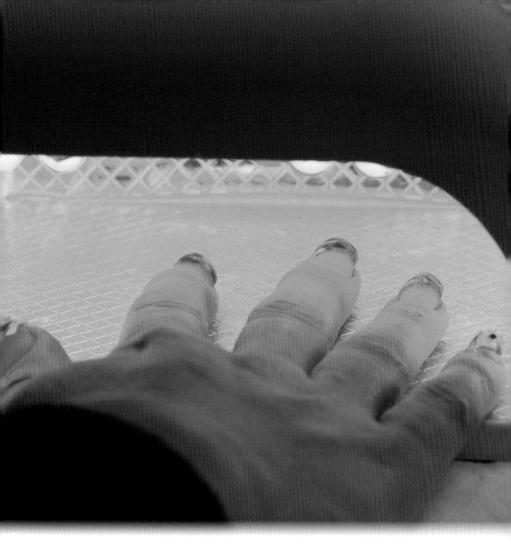

Gel polish is dried under an LED or UV light.

Nail bars

Some people like to put on their own nail polish but more and more people now have their nails done at a nail bar.

3. Nail care

Nail map

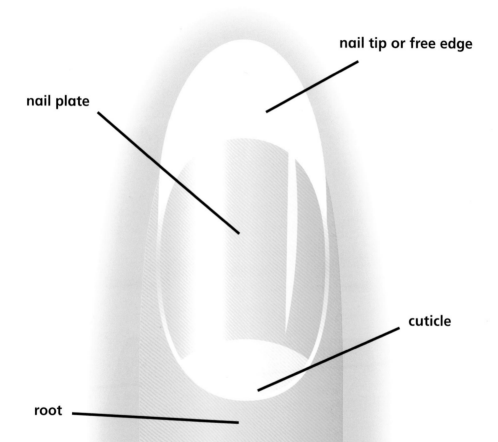

nail tip or free edge

nail plate

cuticle

root

Manicure

A manicure keeps every part of your nails looking good.

To give yourself a manicure:

1. Massage the nail root and cuticle.

2. Tidy the cuticle.

3. File and shape the nail tip.

4. Paint the nails.

French manicure

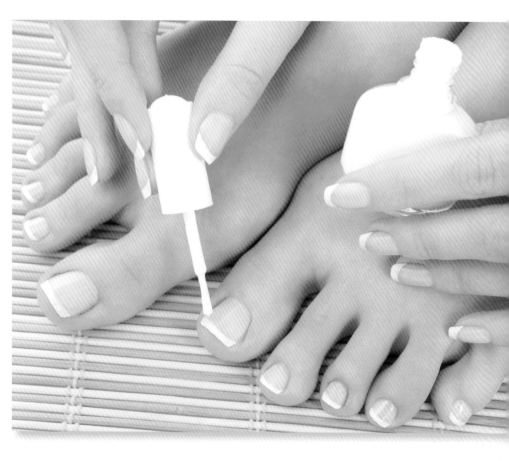

A French manicure uses:
- pink nail polish on the nail plate
- white polish on the nail tip

Nail care dos and don'ts

- Do keep your nails clean and dry.
- Do moisturise your nails.
- Do wear gloves when cleaning or gardening.
- Don't tear hangnails.
- Don't bite your nails.
- Don't use your nails as tools!

The nail plate and tip are dead – which is why it doesn't hurt when you cut your nails!

4. Nail art

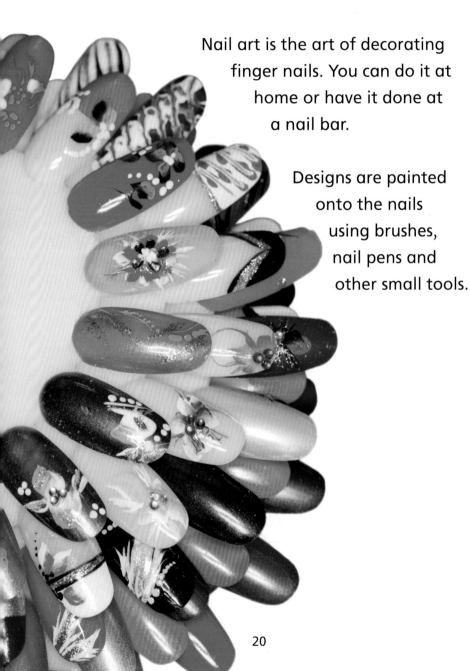

Nail art is the art of decorating finger nails. You can do it at home or have it done at a nail bar.

Designs are painted onto the nails using brushes, nail pens and other small tools.

20

Patterns

Some of the easiest designs to try are dots and stripes.

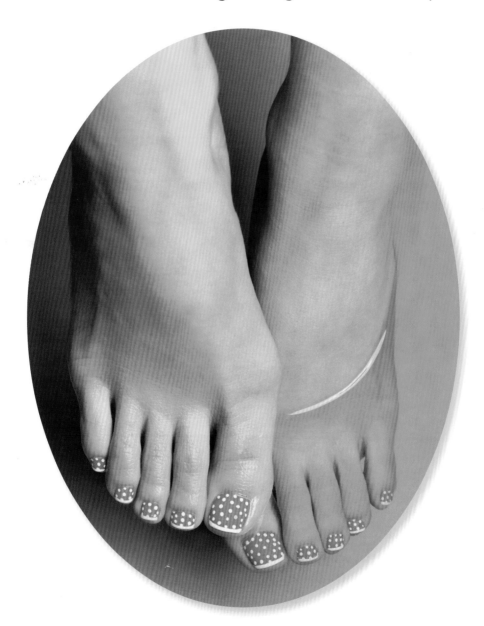

Glitter and shine

Nails can be made to look
sparkly using metallic polish…

…glitter…

…or by sticking
on tiny jewels.

Stickers

A quick way of decorating nails is to use stickers or transfers.

But they need to be painted with nail art sealer to keep them in place.

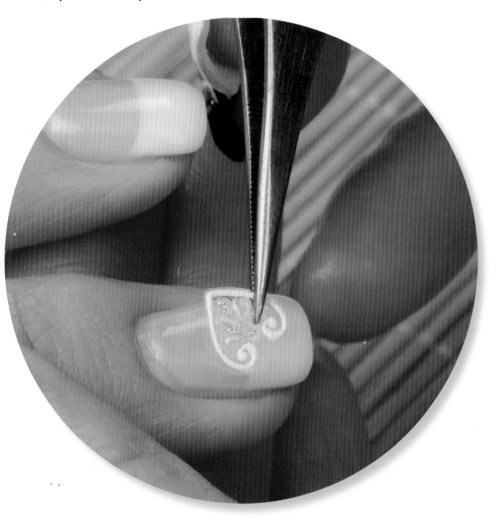

Special days

People sometimes have nail designs done for important days, such as birthdays, Christmas and other special occasions.

This bride has had her nails specially decorated for her wedding day.

WOW! facts

The first false nail was invented in the 1950s by a man whose nail had come off in an accident!

5. Nail facts

The current world record for the longest fingernails is held by Chris Walton from Las Vegas.

Each nail is over 60 centimetres long! It has taken Chris 18 years to grow her nails this long.

But the longest fingernails ever belonged to Melvin Boothe, who died in 2009.

Added together, his nails were almost ten metres long!

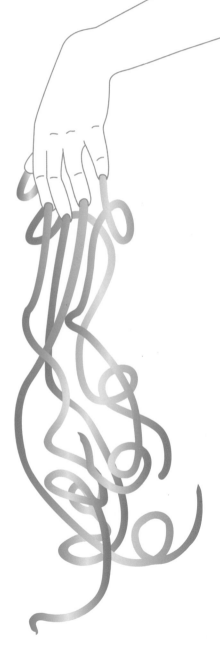

The Nailympics!

You have heard of the Olympics. But have you heard of the Nailympics?

Every year, people from all over the world take part in big nail art competitions.

One of the biggest competitions is held every year in London.

The nail art at these competitions is amazing!

WOW! facts

False nails may look cool but watch out! Lots of bugs may be lurking under long nails!

Five things you never knew about your nails

1. Nails are made of the same stuff as hair, feathers, horns and hooves.

2. Nails grow about one millimetre a week.

3. Nails grow faster in the summer.

4. Men's nails grow faster than women's nails.

5. Fingernails grow twice as fast as toenails.

Questions

The first people to paint their nails lived how long ago? *(page 5)*

What is the name of the dye used in ancient Egypt to colour nails? *(page 6)*

In ancient China, which colours would the most important people paint their nails? *(page 9)*

What colour was the first modern nail polish? *(page 10)*

What is a French manicure? *(page 17)*

What nail art design would you like for yourself?

Index